SEX
IS
COMPLICATED

LET'S TALK ABOUT IT

MIKE NOVOTNY

Published by Straight Talk Books
P.O. Box 301, Milwaukee, WI 53201
800.661.3311 · timeofgrace.org

Printed in the United States of America
ISBN: 978-1-949488-46-3

Contents

Introduction

Sex is complicated. (If you don't believe me, bring up sex at your church's next Bible study!)

For some people, sex is exciting. It's exciting to think that what happens in the marriage bed isn't evil, shameful, or taboo but instead an act of worship designed by the One who is worthy of all our worship. Like Adam and Eve before the fall into sin, many Christian couples are excited to be naked and unashamed.

For other people, sex is interesting. It's interesting to learn how our bodies were created, about the brilliant ways that the Creator wired our brains and our bodies with a stunning connection between nerve endings and pleasure-inducing chemicals. In a world with too much fake news about sex, it's interesting to get back to the biblical basics and learn how, why, and for whom God created sex.

For still other people, sex is bittersweet. It's bittersweet for the widow who misses the warm embrace of her husband's touch. It's bittersweet to long for marriage yet struggle to find the right person to marry. It's bittersweet to be married yet lack sexual intimacy, something that a shocking number of couples experience.

For certain people, sex is triggering. It's triggering to be touched in the present when someone touched you inappropriately in your past. God weeps at the number of his children who have been sexually abused, a sin that shapes the way victims see sex and see themselves.

For others still, sex is urgent. It's urgent when your children and grandchildren are growing up in a world where sex is everywhere, where one sexual encounter can change the direction of their lives, and where today's self-control can lead to a harvest of future blessings that few teenagers will figure out without wise and courageous parents.

Sex is complicated for the Christian church. So what reaction does sex provoke in your heart? Does it inspire you to read on or tempt you to put down this book?

Whatever your story or relationship status, I'm so glad you've given this book a chance, because this is about "us." Not just me. Not just you. But *us*. Christians are called to be part of the "body" of Christ, a metaphor that reminds us that God cares about all of us and that we are called to care about one another.

Which is why, no matter what your personal situation, I believe you need this book, either for yourself or for someone whom you are called to serve. You know someone who finds sex interesting and someone else who finds it bittersweet. You care about a Christian who needs healing from their sexual trauma and another who urgently needs truth in this world of sexual lies. Like the Lord's Prayer itself, this book's purpose is the plural, the *us* who need to know God's will, the *us* who need forgiveness of sins, and the *us* who need to be led not into

As you read, I hope you think about *us*.

temptation but delivered from evil. As you read, I hope you think about *us*, about your friends, family, and brothers and sisters in Christ.

In a previous book, *Sexpectations*, I laid a foundation for a biblical view of sex. Those chapters revealed that sex is good, sex is work, sex is fiery, and sex is unnecessary. If you have not yet read *Sexpectations*, I would encourage you to begin there.

In this supplementary book, I want to take you back over ten years to the first messages I ever shared about sex from God's perspective. Back in 2011, I studied the Bible book of Song of Songs, that unique/poetic/surprising addition to the Old Testament (that deserves a PG-13 rating!). My studies led to four sermons, which now make up the chapters of this book. I originally shared these sermons with *us*, with the local church that I was serving in Madison, Wisconsin.

I was a fairly young pastor at the time, and this was my first attempt at publicly discussing sex from a biblical perspective, so I won't promise you these next chapters are filled with the wisdom that only age and experience can provide. That's why, after you read each one, I would like to slow down and talk to you about it. What did you think about the chapter? Looking back, what do I now think about my decade-old words? These study sections will help you personalize and apply God's Word to your life.

Are you ready to dive in and listen to our loving Father as he speaks to *us*?

All Scripture is God-breathed
and is useful for teaching, rebuking,
correcting and training in righteousness,
so that the servant of God may be
thoroughly equipped for every good work.

2 Timothy 3:16,17

Chapter 1

God Likes Good Sex

Preached February 6, 2011

I have a book that makes people uncomfortable. It's not the Quran or the *Da Vinci Code*. It's a skinny book with a provocative title: *Sex God*. That combination makes people uneasy. We're okay with Prayer God or Giving God, but Sex God just doesn't seem respectful. Likewise, we can say, "God loves sunsets" or, "God loves sharing." But if we say, "God loves sex," people pick up mental stones and accuse us of blasphemy. Sex and God seem like concepts to be kept worlds apart, especially on Sunday morning.

But I wonder if that separation is good for God's people. After all, Sunday morning might be the only time we don't learn about sex. The shows we watch, the Super Bowl ads, and the magazines at the grocery store are more than willing to be our instructors on the subject. The question then isn't if someone will teach you about sex. The question is simply *who* will?

God has always recognized that fact. When he wrote the Old Testament, the first part of the Bible, he knew the Canaanite culture was teaching his people about sex. That culture claimed the gods of nature would send rain from heaven once they had been aroused by sexual acts here on earth. When God wrote the New Testament, he knew the Greek culture was teaching his people about sex. That culture promoted adultery, premarital sex, homosexuality, sex with children, orgies, and temple prostitution. Not surprisingly, the word *sex* appears 77 times in the Bible. God knew his people were being taught about sex constantly. So he talked about sex all the time. He wanted his people to learn from the right Source.

If God wrote us a book today, do you think he'd talk about sex? Is our culture as sex-crazed as the Canaanites and the Greeks? A glance at the checkout aisle might answer that. Have you noticed that most marketing is targeted at making you "sexy"? How to get sexy hair, sexy skin, sexy abs, and how to get the sexiest jeans of the season. Or go online. Statistics tell us *sex-crazed* isn't a strong enough word for our obsession with internet pornography. According to internet safety expert Jerry Ropelato, over $3,000 is spent on internet porn every second, and every second over 28,000 internet users are viewing pornography (http://www.ministry-oftruth.me.uk/wp-content/uploads/2014/03/IFR2007.pdf). That means before I finish this sermon, over 558,000 sex-related searches will be made and over $4.8 million will be spent on internet porn. In 2006 the porn industry made more than MLB, NBA, NFL, and NHL combined. So if you think baseball is America's favorite pastime, you're wrong. According to the authors of *Hooked*, 46% of high school students have had sex and over 70% of graduating seniors have (pages 100,101). On average, a child is first exposed to pornography at age 11, often accidentally as he or she works online for a school project. So statistically, some of the children who leave church today have already seen explicit sexual images. Maybe that's not surprising in a country obsessed with sex.

Stories from pop culture are even more revealing. Abercrombie & Fitch, a popular store for teens, sells shirts that read, "Female students wanted for sexual research." On television, *Jersey Shore* is the number-one rated cable show. (Don't forget; I preached this sermon in 2011!) MTV cast a group of young, sexually charged partygoers; pays for their alcohol; and tapes the results. You don't have to be a fan of the show to guess what happens. Ashleymadison.com is a website devoted to help married people cheat on their spouses. Last year, the company approached the New York Giants and offered them $25 million to rename their stadium Ashleymadison.com Stadium. Fortunately, the Giants declined the offer. Unfortunately, the offer proves business is good for ashleymadison.com. And then there's *Sesame Street*. This year's season premier featured a duet between a well-known pop singer and Elmo. However, when the singer chose her outfit, she apparently forgot *Sesame Street* is for 2-year-olds, not 22-year-olds. The directors and producers taped the show and planned to air it until outraged parents expressed their disbelief over her outfit.

What does this all prove? The Canaanites of the Old Testament and the Greeks of the New Testament got nothing on us. We know sex sells, and apparently everyone is trying to sell something. So if God lovingly talked about sex back then, don't you think he wants to talk about sex with his people today?

Don't you think he wants to talk about sex with his people today?

If you're still not convinced, you need to know this isn't just about "those people out there." This is about God's people "in here." Though you may not talk about purity and pornography in the meet-and-greet session after church, our members are wrestling with sexual issues. Couples have been devastated by adultery. Churchgoing men have admitted addictions to pornography. Christian high school graduates are living together and sleeping together before marriage, despite what they learned from God's Word. I once tried to identify the owner of a cell phone left at church and found naked pictures of the owner's teenage girlfriend.

And, if we're honest, we might admit we don't exactly know how to handle sex. Parents don't know how to talk about it with their kids. Teenagers don't know how to handle the confusion and pressure of high school. Christians wrestle with sexual identity and don't know if they can talk about it or with whom they can talk about it. Married couples accept bland sex lives. And most of us have no clue what God says about these issues.

That's why we're doing this. That's why we need to hear what God says. We know not all of you are married. Some of you aren't yet. Some of you were. Some of you never will be. But we hope you see the need to teach all of God's people about sex. We know many of you never heard a word on godly sexuality. So let's talk about it. Let's open the Scriptures and see the plans God has, not just for our souls but also for our bodies. Let's take something so common in our culture and set it apart as something sacred. Let's sanctify sex.

To do that, we're going to spend four weeks

in a part of the Bible you've probably never read and never heard in church. It's a book that sometimes makes you think and sometimes makes you blush. It's called Song of Songs. This book has been the object of constant discussion as Christians have tried to figure out if this is a real story about life, love, and sex or if this is a metaphor about God's love for his church. The discussion has been so intense that this 6-page book of the Bible is the basis for the largest book I own, a 1,300-page commentary! As we dive in, I will suggest that Song of Songs is a literal description of God's love of good sex and also a subtle message about his spiritual love for people. So are you ready to go?

As we start, notice there are three characters in Song of Songs: The wife (called "She"), the husband (called "He"), and their friends (cleverly named "Friends"). We meet them all from the very start of chapter 1: **"Solomon's Song of Songs. She: Let him kiss me with the kisses of his mouth—for your love is more delightful than wine. Pleasing is the fragrance of your perfumes; your name is like perfume poured out. No wonder the young women love you!**

Take me away with you—let us hurry! Let the king bring me into his chambers. Friends: We rejoice and delight in you; we will praise your love more than wine. She: How right they are to adore you!" (verses 1-4).

Note the author of this book: Solomon. This is not some hormone-fueled frat boy. This is the one God calls the wisest man who ever lived. Note the title of this book: Song of Songs. That's a Hebrew way of saying, "The best song." It's like "Lord of Lords" means "the greatest Lord." The Bible says Solomon wrote 1,005 songs, but this one is the best. This is Solomon's greatest hit.

Note the details of these opening verses: A woman wants to be intimate with her husband. She doesn't say, "Let him pray for me and read a devotion." She says, **"Let him kiss me."** She wants a romantic and passionate moment. Why? **"For your love is more delightful than wine."** The word *love* here refers to lovemaking. This isn't just "sex." This isn't just a physical act. It's emotional. It's personal. It's sacred. It is **"more delightful than wine."** She doesn't want a glass of Merlot. She wants to make love to her husband. For this wife, making love is not a duty; it's a hobby. It's not a requirement for childbearing; it's a recreational pastime!

"Pleasing is the fragrance of your perfumes." Guys, this is God's advice on personal hygiene. By nature, you and I are stinky. If you want a biblical sex life, don't be stinky. Take a shower. Buy deodorant (and use it). Have her pick out a cologne she likes. **"Your name is like perfume poured out."** Ah, this is even more important. In the Bible, a person's name was their character, their reputation. This wife wants to be with her husband because his character is sweet "like perfume." She likes thinking about his name, the way he treats her, the way he loves God and loves her. **"Take me away with you—let us hurry!"** She's excited about sex. This is a man she loves and a man who loves her. That love makes her want to make love.

And here's the main point for today: God doesn't object. God doesn't jump in and scream, "Hey! This is the Bible! You can't talk like that! 'Kiss me?!?' 'Take me away?!?' Do you think this is late-night TV?" No, not a word of that from

God. In fact, God inspired this. The Holy Spirit guided Solomon to write these very words. That fact will shock you if you take five minutes to read all of Song of Songs. The sensual language. The sexual imagery. The phrases that make you think, "Wait. Is that saying what I think it's saying?"

Is that saying what I think it's saying?

Why would God inspire a book like this? Because sex was God's idea! God invented sex. God holds the patent on the act. God drew up the blueprints for our bodies. The proof is in paradise. Back in the Garden of Eden when everything was perfect, God created man and woman, united them in marriage, and said, **"They become one flesh"** (Genesis 2:24). Jesus went back to that perfect design when he talked about starting a new family through marriage and becoming **"one flesh"** with your spouse (Mark 10:8). First Corinthians 6:16 tells us **"one flesh"** is not just a metaphor for family life. It's a reference to the physical act of making love. Simply put—God likes good sex. God likes it when you help the poor. God likes it when you forgive your enemies. And God likes it when spouses enjoy the wedding gift he designed and gave. God likes good sex.

Maybe that sentence makes you uncomfortable because Christians warn people about sex more than they praise it. But Song of Songs allows us to be sexual optimists and celebrate sex as a gift from God. Others have done that. Traditionally, Song of Songs was one of the five books the Jewish people read during holy days and religious festivals. That would be like us reading it during a Christmas Eve service! But to the Jews, there was no disconnect. "We're worshiping God for his gifts. Sex is a gift from God. So why not worship God for giving us sex?!"

Song of Songs allows us to be sexual optimists.

As pastors, teachers, parents, and friends, we need to balance our warnings about bad, sinful sex with a celebration of good, godly sex. I think, historically, churches have emphasized the former: "Don't have sex until you're married." "It's sinful for you to have sex now." "Don't look at pornography!" Are these warnings appropriate? Yes, because God hates bad sex. He says just like he will judge thieves and gossips and racists, he will judge adulterers and the sexually immoral. God hates it when we set our bodies up as idols and worship what feels good instead of what God says is good. He hates it when teenagers tear open the present God intended for their wedding night. He hates it when spouses cheat, people look at porn, and couples consensually sin against his design for sex. God commands us to repent of sexual sin, because she might be hot but so is hell, and that's where unrepentant body worshipers go.

But don't forget the symbolic message of Song of Songs. More than this husband loves his wife, God loves us. That man's **"name is like perfume poured out,"** but the name of Jesus is even sweeter. Jesus has pursued us more than a lovestruck husband pursues his wife. Jesus' love is more delightful than wine. Not his sexual love, but his selfless love, which led him to a cross. There Jesus cleansed us from impurity. There Jesus covered the stains of our sexual sins. There Jesus took away the shame of late nights online and the guilt of premarital sex. At the cross Jesus gave us a new outfit to wear—a pure, white, spotless outfit called righteousness. Like a bride in a shimmering dress, God has made us beautiful in his sight. And just as a man holds his breath as his bride walks down the aisle, heaven holds its breath as it realizes what Jesus has made you. You are not dirty in God's sight. You are not a deviant. You are not impure. Through faith in Christ, you are cleansed, perfect, and pure.

As God's sanctified people, we can balance our warnings about sex with our celebration of it. We can praise it as the sacred gift that it is. Parents, can I encourage you, at the appropriate age, to give your kids a godly perspective on sex? Be Genesis chapters 1 and 2 parents. Genesis chapter 1 parents say God made the man and the woman and the birds and the bees. Genesis chapters 1 and 2 parents go on to teach their kids about the man and the woman and the birds and the bees. Not just the biology but the theology. Teach your kids God likes good sex.

Finally, let's rescue sex from our culture and restore it to the place God intended it to be. Let's remember our sexuality is like fine china. Fine china is set apart in a special place. It's protected and handled with care. You can toss around paper plates and toss them out after dinner, but not china.

China is for special occasions. Your sexuality is like that. Don't treat

Don't secularize your sexuality. Sanctify it.

it as a paper plate you pull out on the third date. No, set it apart for someone special. Protect it. Handle it with care. Don't secularize your sexuality. Sanctify it. Don't give it away to every girl with a pulse or every guy who tells you he loves you or to every online fantasy. Set it apart as something sacred just like God does. Because you are sacred. Your body is sacred. And because God loves good sex.

Study Questions

1. What two to three ideas/paragraphs/points jumped out at you as you read this chapter? Why do you suppose those particular ideas stood out?

2. My goal in this first sermon was to persuade *us* (a church filled with singles, couples, divorced people, and widows) that *we* needed to talk about sex. Do you think I succeeded? Why or why not? What might have made the message even more persuasive?

3. After preaching this message, I recall one young man saying, "This is the best series we have ever had at church." One older man (whom I greatly respected) said, "Don't you think that this had too much advice and not enough good news about Jesus' forgiveness?" Looking back at the final paragraphs of the message, do you think I gave too little space to the love and mercy of Jesus? (I tend to think so, but I wonder if you felt spiritually burdened or comforted by the end of the sermon.)

4. As you stay focused on *us*, who are two people in your life who could really use this message? How might you share it with them in the wisest way?

Chapter 2

Godly Sex Is Selfless

Preached February 13, 2011

Good sex does not come naturally. If you need proof, just walk down any checkout aisle. There you won't see a magazine article titled, "The 5 Secret Tips on How to Walk." *Cosmo* won't have the headline, "3 Ways to Breathe Better Than Ever Before." *Men's Health* will never grab your attention with, "The 1 Thing Every Woman Wishes Her Man Knew About Being Tall." Why don't you see headlines like that? Because that stuff comes naturally. You don't need an article on how to walk or breathe or grow. Those things just happen.

But good sex is different. It doesn't just happen. Maybe that's why every magazine besides *Better Homes and Gardens* wants to teach you how to make it happen. "5 Secret Tips for a Great Love Life," "3 Ways to Spice Up Your

Marriage," "The 1 Thing She Wishes You Knew About Sex." Every editor wants to sell you the secret to good sex. But we would be gullible if we believed *Cosmo* knew better than the cosmic Creator-God. After all, if sex is God's good gift, then shouldn't God know what makes sex good? That's what today's Scripture is all about.

We pick up King Solomon's wise words about life, love, sex, and God in Song of Songs 2:14. The husband speaks to his wife: **"My dove in the clefts of the rock, in the hiding places on the mountainside, show me your face, let me hear your voice; for your voice is sweet, and your face is lovely."** And all the ladies said, "Awwww!" Here is a husband who is selfless with his words. He pours out compliments to his wife. Modern psychologists call these words of affirmation. **"My dove . . . your voice is sweet . . . your face is lovely."** This guy takes the time to make his wife feel beautiful.

If you read this entire Song, you'll feel like you're eavesdropping on two lovestruck kids. The compliments outnumber the verses: **"Your name is like perfume . . . No wonder the young women love you . . . How right they** are to adore you . . . How beautiful you are, my darling . . . How handsome you are, my beloved . . . My beloved is like a young stag . . . My beloved is to me a cluster of henna blossoms from the vineyards of En Gedi (I went to En Gedi in Israel—it's a green oasis in the middle of a brown desert. Waterfalls gush and flowers burst with life. "That's how my husband is," this wife says.) . . . Your hair is like a flock of goats descending from the hills of Gilead (That's romantic! Mt. Gilead is on the other side of the Jordan River. Goats with midnight black fur run down its hills. Picture a Pantene commercial where beautiful black hair flows down a woman's back. "That's how my wife is," this husband says.) . . . Your head crowns you like Mount Carmel (That's a lush mountain on the Mediterranean Coast.) . . . There is no flaw in you . . . You are a garden . . . His body is like polished ivory . . . His arms are rods of gold . . . My dove, my perfect one, is unique."

Now there's a secret to a great love life! Does it surprise you this couple enjoyed being intimate? They made each other feel wanted, desired, beautiful. God wants the same for us. Ephesians 4:29 says the words we speak should build each other up. So compliment your spouse. What do you like about her? Her cute nose? Her big brown eyes? Her soft hair? Her figure? His cologne? His arms? His six-pack? His one-pack? His smile? Then say it. Don't assume she knows: "I told you that you were beautiful in 1987! Did you forget?!?" No, say it again and again and again. In a culture where advertisers are constantly telling you what you need to fix about your body, be the one who tells your spouse, "I love

Be selfless with your words.

your body. Don't listen to them. I'm the one who said, 'Until death do us part,' and I think you're gorgeous." Be selfless with your words.

There are a lot of crummy songs on the radio these days, but there's one pop song you need to download during this week. It's by an R & B singer named Bruno Mars, and it's called "Just the Way You Are." Check out the lyrics! (I think he read Song of Songs before writing those selfless words.)

Next Solomon points us to selfless actions:

"Catch for us the foxes, the little foxes that ruin the vineyards, our vineyards that are in bloom" (Song of Songs 2:15). Every gardener here gets that. One little animal, one hungry baby bunny, can ruin your garden. If you don't build a fence and evict all animals currently residing there, your garden will be gone. But Solomon isn't really thinking about gardens here. In Song of Songs, "vineyards" is often a reference to a person's sexuality or a couple's love life. And wise Solomon, just like the magazine editors, knows "little foxes" can ruin God's good gift of sex. What are these foxes? They're anything that destroys the passion of a good sex life.

Every married couple could think of the foxes they've found in their marriage vineyard. Busyness is a fox. When you're worn out from work and errands and commitments, who has the time or energy to make love? Stress is a fox. When your mind is so focused on what you have to do tomorrow that you forget about what you could do tonight. Little kids can be little foxes. They demand 25 hours of attention each day and seem to be oblivious that if Mommy and

Daddy didn't have a sex life, they wouldn't be here in the first place! Selfish words are little foxes. A lot of insults make for a lot of lonely nights. Past events can be a big fox. Abuse, molestation, and rape can twist sex into something emotionally painful. Selfish actions can be a fox. She shoots him down because his needs aren't her biggest priority. He multiplies the problem by not realizing she may not want sex every night. Little foxes are everywhere, and they can ruin the vineyard of a good, godly sex life.

Little foxes are everywhere.

So what should couples do? Solomon commands, "Catch the foxes!" Just like you'd protect your garden from rabbits, protect your bed from things that destroy it. And just like catching a real fox, catching these foxes is not easy. It takes work. It takes honest communication. But the work is worth it. It will save you from a passionless marriage. Catch the fox of busyness. Limit your commitments and leagues and extracurriculars if you're too drained.

Catch the fox of stress. Read Jesus' words

on not worrying about the future you can't control so you can enjoy the present moment you can control.

Catch the fox of children. Put them up for adoption (just kidding!). This one is tough. Maybe the key is to be first a good spouse and then a good parent. Because being a good parent first can rob us of the energy needed to be a good spouse. And I believe kids don't really need parents who cater to their needs every minute. I believe kids need to see their parents crazy in love with each other. They need to see Daddy kissing Mommy and hear Mommy complimenting Daddy. They need Daddy to take Mommy on dates and Mommy to budget for babysitters. They need a model for relationships, romance, and love. Be a good spouse first.

Catch the fox of selfishness. Repent before God and before your spouse if you've put your wants over his or her needs. Look to the cross and see how selfless God has been in cleansing you of selfish sins. Ask God for the power to give and serve and be selfless in marriage. Catch all the foxes that will ruin your love life. That's your homework if you're married. Ask your spouse what the foxes are in your marriage and come up with a plan to catch them.

Think of your sex life as a garden. Jesus once told a story about a man who had a garden vineyard: **"He put a wall around it, dug a winepress in it and built a watchtower"** (Matthew 21:33). I saw an example of that in Nazareth. Nazareth Village is a modern reconstruction of what a first-century village might have looked like. In the middle of the village stands a stone watchtower. High above, a watchman keeps his eyes peeled for anything and anyone that could ruin the vineyard below.

Your sex life needs a watchman *and* a watchwoman, spouses who will take an honest look at what's sneaking into the

Be selfless with your actions.

vineyard. Spouses who are selflessly willing to catch the foxes and set that vineyard apart as something sacred.

Be selfless with your words. Be selfless with your actions. Finally, Solomon tells us to be selfless with our bodies: **"My beloved is mine and I am his; he browses among the lilies. Until the day breaks and the shadows** flee, turn, my beloved, and be like a gazelle or like a young stag on the rugged hills"** (Song of Songs 2:16,17). That's selfless. **"My beloved is mine and I am his."** This couple doesn't just have a joint checking account. They have joint ownership of each other's bodies. That's just what the apostle Paul taught us in 1 Corinthians 7:4,5: **"The wife does not have authority over her own body but yields it to her husband. In the same way, the husband does not have authority over his own body but yields it to his wife. Do not deprive each other except perhaps by mutual consent and for a time."**

Solomon and Paul knew this important fact: A husband has no godly place to be sexually fulfilled besides his wife. And a wife has no godly place to be sexually fulfilled besides her husband. God has not opened up any other "gardens" for your spouse. Adultery is sinful. Open marriages are sinful. Pornography is sinful. If your spouse is going to enjoy God's wedding gift, he can only do it with you. That's why these words are so important for every couple. **"My beloved is mine and I am his."** Practically, that means being selfless with your sexuality. It means going out of your way to please her even if it's not the perfect time for you. It means going out of your way to satisfy him even if you're not in the mood. It means taking the selfless call of Christian living and bringing it into your bedroom.

You can't do that without Christ's help and the Holy Spirit's power. Jesus never had sex, but he had a life filled with selfless moments. His every breath was selflessly given for us. He selflessly lived a pure life and selflessly died a pure death for us. He caught the little foxes of sin that ruined our spiritual lives and kicked them out by forgiving our sins. He cared for us by giving us Baptism and the Lord's Supper so we could burst with spiritual life; so we could put others first; so we could be selfless at work, in the kitchen, and in the bedroom.

Brothers and sisters in Christ, this is the key to a godly sex life. So ignore the magazines. Just read your Bible. Let God teach you about his selfless love and inspire you to be selfless with your words, your actions, and your body.

Study Questions

1. My gut reaction to reading this sermon was how I rushed a small paragraph of Jesus' love in at the end, further convincing me that the feedback I received from that older gentleman (see page 26) was valid. As you skim over the chapter/sermon, what other opportunities did I have to connect these words to the forgiving work of Jesus?

2. The concept of "little foxes" stuck with me after seeing a marriage workshop based off the Song of Songs. Which of the examples cause the most trouble among you, your family, and your friends? In other words, which issues drive couples apart from the emotional intimacy that leads to the best sexual connections?

3. Evaluate: "First be a good spouse; then be a good parent."

4. In my counseling experience, struggling couples never have good sex lives. Why do you suppose that is? Would you agree that sex is a litmus test for a healthy, selfless relationship? Why or why not?

5. Once again, think about how this message applies to *us*. Take five minutes in prayer, asking our Father to forgive our sins, fill our mouths with affirming words, and give us wisdom to rid our relationships of little foxes.

Chapter 3

God Likes ~~Safe~~ ~~Safer~~ the Safest Sex

Preached February 20, 2011

We should practice safe sex. If there's one thing most Americans see eye to eye on, it's that. Our legal system agrees—Dangerous sex with a minor or without consent can get you sentenced for life. Our medical system agrees—Dangerous sex without an exam can get you an STD. Our educational system agrees—Dangerous sex without protection can result in an unplanned pregnancy. Safe sex is a core value of our sex-obsessed culture. You can have casual sex, premarital sex, same-sex sex, online sex, one-night-stand sex, multiple-partner sex, and whatever other kind of sex you can think of . . . just as long as no one gets hurt, just as long as the sex is safe.

But one morning Americans woke up

and admitted: Safe sex is a myth. Checking her ID, getting tested, and using protection can't guarantee sex will be safe. That's why

Safe sex is a myth.

organizations like Planned Parenthood have added one letter to the famous phrase. Safe sex is now called *Safer* sex. Follow these steps, they say, and sex will be safer than it would be if you didn't.

Safer. Adding one little letter *r* reminds us *safer* is a subjective word. Safer than what? Safer according to whom? If sex can be dangerous, who determines what makes it safe? Planned Parenthood? Your parents? Your doctors? Your sex education teacher? Your church? If you value safety in your sexuality, whose definition of *safe* will you believe?

Today's reading is one of many Scriptures that give us God's definition of safe sex. We've been studying Solomon's Song of Songs, the book of the Bible filled with God's view of sexuality. From the start, we've admitted this is a challenging book. But this much is clear: In the parts we will read here, the passion we saw between this man and his wife is missing . . .

"**She: I slept but my heart was awake. Listen! My beloved is knocking: 'Open to me, my sister, my darling, my dove, my flawless one. My head is drenched with dew, my hair with the dampness of the night'**" (Song of Songs 5:2). A husband comes calling for his wife. It's the perfect time to make love, so he initiates. But this time there's a problem. She's already in bed. Undressed. Face washed. Makeup off. Half asleep. Picture a woman in the sweatpants she's had longer than her husband. Glasses on. Eyes drooping as she reads in her cozy bed. Suddenly, her cell buzzes on the nightstand. It's her husband. "Honey, it's me. I know it's late, but I just got off work and I've been thinking about you all day. I picked up some wine, and these flowers next to me have your name on them. Why don't you meet me at the door in something special, and we'll see what happens . . ." She glances at her sweatpants and the clock. "Ugh. Sweetie, do you know what time it is? I'm already in bed. Why don't you put the wine in the fridge. Maybe another night." Or, the Song says in B.C. terms, "**I have taken off my robe—must I put it on again? I have** washed my feet—must I soil them again?" (verse 3). Simple translation: "Not in the mood." But he is. Verse 4: **"My beloved thrust his hand through the latch-opening."** He reaches out to her, but she doesn't reach back.

Within a minute, the pounding on the door stops, but another pounding begins: **"My heart began to pound for him"** (verse 4). Sex started to simmer in her mind. Maybe it would be worth the work. Maybe it would be fun. Maybe her husband was really looking forward to it. So she gets up and runs to the bathroom—changes into something he likes, spritzes his favorite perfume, puts sweet lotion on her hands. **"I arose to open for my beloved, and my hands dripped with myrrh"** (verse 5). She races down the stairs, picturing his face when he sees her in this, when he smells her, when he kisses her. She reaches for the door. **"My fingers with flowing myrrh, on the handles of the bolt"** (verse 5). She fixes her hair and swings the door open. **"I opened for my beloved, but my beloved had left; he was gone. My heart sank at his departure"** (verse 6). Gone. Why? Frustrated? Shot down? Angry? She doesn't know.

Where to? Work? Out with the guys? Into the arms of another? She doesn't know. But she knows she misses him.

Now her heart beats with worry and love. **"I looked for him but did not find him. I called him but he did not answer"** (verse 6). She goes to his favorite spots. No luck. Calls his cell. No answer. But before she can find him, someone else finds her: **"The watchmen found me as they made their rounds in the city"** (verse 7). Watchmen patrol the city walls and keep their eyes peeled for wrongdoers. But tonight they are the ones doing wrong. **"They beat me, they bruised me; they took away my cloak, those watchmen of the walls!"** (verse 7). What's happening? Are they abusing her? Robbing her? Raping her? We don't know. But we do know it is an ugly night for this pretty woman.

Sin makes sex unsafe.

She calls out in her distress: **"Daughters of Jerusalem, I charge you—if you find my beloved, what will you tell him? Tell him I am faint with love"** (verse 8).

The story is somewhat confusing, but the moral is clear—Sin makes sex unsafe. The once selfless wife selfishly thinks of herself. The once selfless husband selfishly vanishes, leaving his wife alone and afraid. The once heroic watchmen turn into villains, hurting an innocent woman. Feelings are hurt. Love is squelched. Passion is gone. And stuck in the middle of this sensual story is a cold counseling moment. Sin makes sex dangerous.

God wants us to consider that statement. Fast-forward past the pleasure of the evening and look at the morning after. Is sinful sex dangerous? Has violating God's design for sex been safe for our culture? Are we happier, healthier, and more blessed because of casual sex? I don't think we are. The staggering number of women and children who have been raped and abused is not safe. According to the National Institute of Justice, one in six American women has been raped. That's like having every baby girl roll a die, and each one who rolls a 1 will be raped. That means, statistically, over 40 rape victims come to church here each weekend. The stunning number of teens with sexually transmitted diseases is not safe. According to the Centers for Disease Control and Prevention, one in four

American girls ages 14-19 has an STD. That's at least one starter on *every* high school girls basketball team in the nation. The shocking number of children who don't know their own fathers is not safe.

Like the child I met last December. "What do you want for Christmas?" I asked, expecting him to rattle off a list of action figures and video games.

"All I want," he groaned as he stared at the ground, "is to see my dad. I haven't seen him in years."

The appalling number of spouses addicted to pornography is not safe. The unrealistic expectations porn brings into a marriage bed is not safe. The pressure wives feel to compete with a digital fantasy is not safe. The pain a woman feels when her husband is gawking at skinnier, sexier women is not safe. The rising numbers of sexual partners is not safe. Chemically, our bodies bond through sex. But have sex with enough people, and the bond loses its grip. Like tape that's been reused a dozen times, sex loses its ability to bond you to your future spouse. The outrageous number of sexually selfish spouses is not safe. She doesn't bother to think she is the only godly option for her husband sexually. He doesn't bother to think maybe she doesn't want sex every other second of the day. The devastating number of adulteries is not safe. I have seen the confusion and pain after infidelity comes out of hiding. It tears you apart just to see it, much less to be the victim of it.

Walk toward sinful sex and you walk away from God.

The constant temptation to lust is not safe. Jesus told us lusting can destroy more than our bodies. It can condemn our souls. The rising number of unmarried sexually active people is not safe. The apostle Paul said, **"Anyone who rejects this instruction** [about controlling your body in a holy way] **does not reject a human being but God"** (1 Thessalonians 4:8. Walk toward sinful sex and you walk away from God.

Is all of that safe? Or safer? Than what? A little fish once swam with his dad looking for a bite to eat. As they slalomed through seaweed, the little fish spotted something in the distance. A worm! Just big enough for breakfast.

He darted through the blue-green waters as he moved in on his catch. The closer he got, the bigger and tastier the worm looked. With one last flip of his fin, he opened his mouth wide for his first bite. But just before he chomped down, his father crashed into him! Stunned, the little fish screamed, "Dad! That's my breakfast!"

"No, Son," Dad called back, "that's a trick."

"But, Dad," the little fish protested, "I'm so hungry."

"I know, Son, but it's still a trick."

"But you told me worms are good."

"Not this one, Son. Look there." The little fish looked above the tasty worm and there was a tiny white line leading up to the surface. "Worms are good, Son, but not this one. This one is dangerous."

Sex is good. But not all sex. Sinful sex is dangerous. A pill and her consent won't make sex safe. She may be 18. You may have protection. It may just be a website. You may really feel in love. It might just be this one time. But can we honestly look around at our broken homes, our broken bodies, our broken marriages, and our broken children and admit that our culture's definition of *safe* isn't safe enough? Can we admit maybe God knows more than we do? Can we accept God definition of safe sex—one man, one woman, in marriage, selflessly given?

We need more than safe sex. We need more than safer sex. We need the safest sex. Safest sex is sex according to God's design. Safest sex tells us about our bodies. But it starts by telling us about our souls. It starts with the

Safest sex is sex according to God's design.

story of Jesus. In John chapter 8, Jesus meets a woman who took the bait. Caught cheating, not just by her husband but by the church leaders. These hypocritical and cruel men want her dead, so they drag her to Jesus. Confessing to your husband is hard. Confessing to the church is harder. But confessing to Jesus? Jesus sends her accusers away so just she and he stand there alone. A stained and sinful woman. The pure and perfect Son of God. What will he say? As she stares at him with regret and fear, what will he do? She holds her breath as he opens his mouth, **"Neither do I condemn you. . . . Go now and leave your life of sin"** (John 8:11).

We stand here today with that woman, in danger because of our sexual sins. But today Jesus speaks words of safety and salvation. Looking you in the eye, he swears, "Neither do I condemn you. I did not come into the world to condemn it but to save it. See my hands. See where the nails went through. I was pierced for your sins. I died for the bait you bit so you wouldn't have to. Listen. Listen! God was mad about your sin. Dangerously mad. But God also loved you too much to stay mad. So this was our plan: I came for you. I lived for you so God would never abuse you, leave you, or walk out on you. I was condemned on a cross so you never would be. I came back to life. I rose again so you could have life too—the life that is truly life. The spiritual and not just the physical. The eternal and not just the temporal. I don't condemn you. God doesn't condemn you. You are safe with me."

"Go now and leave your life of sin." Keep your eyes on the cross and believe that the God who invented sex knows what makes it safe. Believe that the God who generously gave his own Son for you loves you enough to set boundaries to protect you. And with the Bible always open in your mind, remember to focus not on the feeling of the attraction but the future of the action. That will keep you safe.

The first time I studied Spanish in Mexico, I had the chance to cheat on my new bride. The college kids from my host family threw me a party. At one point, one of the guys asked me which one of the girls I wanted to sleep with. He said I could pick. (For the record, I played tennis in high school, so this was not a common situation for me!) I told him, "No, man. I'm married."

"Come on!" he yelled over the music. "She's in America."

I showed him my ring.

He shook his head, "You don't know what you're missing."

But I think I did know. By choosing God's safest sex, I was missing out . . . on the guilt, the shame, and the embarrassment of infidelity. I was missing out on the heart-crushing confession to my wife, Kim. I was missing out on a possible divorce. Yeah, maybe I missed out on a fun night in Mexico, but I gained seven years (and counting) of an excellent marriage.

I wish I was always that strong when it comes to sexual temptation. Like you, I've seen and thought a lot of things I shouldn't have. But with Jesus' cleansing forgiveness and the power of the Holy Spirit, we can control what we do today with our bodies. We can focus on the future and not just the feelings of the moment. We can choose purity over a pop-up ad. We can choose to set our bodies aside for the one who will be there until death do us part over the one who just wants us for the night. With God's help, we don't have to live dangerously with our sexuality. We can enjoy the safest sex, just like God designed it.

Study Questions

1. Evaluate: God's rules for sex make life worse today and much better tomorrow.

2. As you think back on your own sexual history, which moments do you regret? Which moments are you proud of? Take a moment to talk with our Father, thanking him for the forgiveness that saves you from shame and for the strength that saved you from the consequences of sexual sin.

3. Challenge: Can you name at least three sexual sinners who were loved, forgiven, and saved by God in the Bible?

4. Whom do you know who is living in a sexually sinful and, therefore, spiritually dangerous situation? How could you help them in a way that balances truth and unconditional love?

5. As you prepare for the final chapter in this book, read the entire book of Song of Songs. It should only take about 20 minutes, and it will both review what we have studied and give you some solid context for the book's conclusion.

Chapter 4
God Likes Committed Sex
Preached February 27, 2011

Sanctifying your sexuality is like acing your SAT. It's uncommon. In our culture, it's challenging to, as the apostle Paul said it, **"learn to control your own body in a way that is holy and honorable"** (1 Thessalonians 4:4). Teens who have boyfriends without benefits are atypical. Guys who've never looked at porn are the exception, not the rule. Purity and chastity are endangered species. So what will we do about it? Consider a solution? Or commit to one? This next section of Song of Songs has the answer . . .

At the end of Song of Songs, we find these words: **"Place me like a seal over your heart, like a seal on your arm"** (8:6). Here a woman is speaking to her husband. She says, "Make me the official owner of all you are. Promise me you'll love me, think about me, consider my needs, and remember how I feel. There are billions of women on this planet, but I want you to identify and commit your heart to just one—me." She has another request: **"Place me like a seal on your arm."** "No one can see your heart, so place my seal on your arm. Don't hide our love. Don't be ashamed of me. No. Talk about me. Be proud of us. Make a visible commitment to our love."

I played basketball the other night with a guy who had a tattoo on his neck. From a distance it looked like a circle with some scribbles next to it. Since it's not cool for a guy to stare at another guy's neck, I had to sneak a quick glance subtly. But I finally figured it out. The scribbles were a name in cursive, the name of his wife. The circle was a red outline of her lips. This husband was not ashamed of his wife! He literally had a "seal," a statement to the world about the owner of his heart and his body.

God is placing his seal on your heart.

Even though many of you are single, these words still apply. Make an inward and outward commitment to purity. God is placing his seal on your heart, setting you apart as his holy child. Take that inward desire of your new man and make it outwardly evident. The apostle Paul says, **"Among you there must not even be a hint of sexual immorality"** (Ephesians 5:3). Why? Because we've taken the outward measures to flee from it.

As the people of God, we have the power to make a commitment today. And we need a commitment to conquer. Since we can't sanctify our sinful world or our sinful nature, we need to sanctify our bodies and minds. So will we?

A young husband named Eric stormed into his pastor's office. "I'm really mad at God," he growled.

"Why?" the pastor wondered.

"Because," Eric fumed, "I looked at porn again."

"Okay," the pastor questioned, "I can see why God would be mad at you. But why are you mad at God?"

Eric explained, "For the last few months, I've been checking out some adult websites. So I prayed and prayed and prayed. I begged, 'God, keep me from sexual immorality.'"

The pastor nodded, "Did you ask anyone to check in on you? Did your wife put a password on your computer?"

"Well . . . no. I didn't want to tell anybody."

The pastor took a book from his shelf and placed it flat on his desk. He started pushing it toward the edge of the desk, inch by inch. As he pushed, he prayed, "O Lord, please keep this book from falling!" But he kept pushing. And kept praying. "O Lord, please keep this book from falling." But soon enough the book tumbled over the edge. God didn't suspend the laws of gravity for the book. And he didn't suspend the laws of purity for this uncommitted man.

Perhaps the most troubling thing isn't what's on the internet. Perhaps the most troubling thing isn't how many Christians sin sexually. Perhaps the most troubling thing is what some Christians do the morning after. Like Eric, too many people expect God to change the laws of nature. The downstairs computer, hidden from Mom's eyes, leads a teen into temptation. But the next morning, it stays downstairs, hidden from Mom's eyes. The swimsuit issue that sparked lust last spring arrives in the same mailbox this year. The boyfriend who took things too far last weekend invites his girlfriend over this weekend, and she goes. Should we be surprised gravity still works?

The answer to our lack of commitment is God's commitment to us. Jesus didn't just think about saving us. He got up and did it. The road to hell may be paved with good intentions,

The road to heaven is paved with the good actions of Jesus Christ.

but the road to heaven is paved with the good actions of Jesus Christ. His committed love is described perfectly here: **"For love is as strong as death, its jealousy unyielding as the grave. It burns like blazing fire, like a mighty flame. Many waters cannot quench love; rivers cannot sweep it away. If one were to give all the wealth of one's house for love, it would be utterly scorned"** (Song of Songs 8:6,7). God's love for us is strong and unyielding. Just like the grave won't give up its dead, God won't give up on us. He is possessive of his people. That's why God sent his only Son. The pure Son of God became impure on the cross, taking on his holy body our unholy sins. But when he died, we, the impure, became something we were not— purified! **"Many waters cannot quench love."** And our many sins cannot extinguish the inferno of God's grace. The massive number of our sins cannot conquer the size of God's love for us. His unending grace is proof of his seal, his commitment to us.

That commitment empowers us to make our commitment, to leave yesterday's apathy and pursue today's purity. So what commitment do you need to make today? What steps do you have to take to be sexually pure? God gives some excellent advice through a man named Job. Job said, **"I made a covenant with my eyes not to look lustfully at a young woman"** (Job 31:1). A covenant. He took purity seriously. Make a covenant with your eyes not to lust. Tell your dad to grab the remote and change the channel whenever a Victoria's Secret commercial comes on. Tell your best friend to punch you if you're checking out a magazine you shouldn't. Ask your sister to ask you each month about your purity and your relationship. Make a covenant. Make a commitment.

If you struggle with pornography, remember gravity works. So make a covenant not to lust and make a change. Put your computer in a public place. Have your mom put a password on it so you can only use it when she's around. If you still can't resist, unplug it and throw your computer in a local lake. Checking your friends' Facebook status is not worth your purity. Get rid of the temptation. Get an accountability partner. Be like Joseph from the Bible who refused to sleep with his boss' wife or even be with her. Don't walk back into the same routine and expect purity to just happen. It won't. Run from it. Commit to being a runner. Flee from sexual temptation. Set your body aside for the one who will one day promise, "Until death do us part." Keep your eyes on the cross, where you'll find power to live for God and the assurance that his plan for your body is best.

So, my fellow Christians, purified by the blood of Christ, don't wait until tomorrow. Don't push your body to the edge and pray you won't fall. No, look to Christ. Make a call. Tell a friend. Get committed. Sanctify your sexuality.

Study Questions

1. I noticed that most (all?) of my examples about pornography were written to/about men. Why was this a foolish choice of words? Why do wise Christians not assume that "that sin" is only committed by "those people"?

2. This message once again touched on the passionate love of Jesus whose love is always greater than our sins. Why is it necessary to talk about grace/mercy/forgiveness/Jesus *every* time we address issues of sexual purity?

3. As you think back on all four chapters/sermons, which truths will stick with you in the days to come? Make a list of your top three takeaways from this study.

4. As you continue to think about *us*, to whom could you give this book? If your notes are too personal, consider picking up a copy for a friend, sibling, child, godchild, etc. so God's Word shapes more and more of "our" minds and hearts.

Conclusion

Sex is indeed complicated. But that's not all it is. For God's people, sex is much, much more than that.

For those who believe in God the Father, the Maker of heaven and earth, sex is a masterpiece. Hands, lips, and minds (and much more!) combine to release unseen chemicals that spark pleasure and bring couples closer together.

For those who believe in God the Son, the Lamb of God who takes away the sins of the world, sex is beautiful. There is nothing we have done or said or thought (or had done to us) that needs to leave us feeling guilty, ashamed, and unworthy. Through Jesus, we are pure, holy, and a delight to God, no matter what our sexual history.

For those who believe in God the Spirit, the producer of love, patience, and self-control, sex is powerful. Singles can be patient as they wait for their wedding days. Divorced people and widows and widowers can be satisfied, knowing that in Jesus they already have something infinitely better than sex. Married couples can make love as a way to express love, a glimpse of the selfless heart that they first saw in their Savior.

So let *us* worship God together for sex, one of the many **"good and perfect gifts"** that come from above (James 1:17).

About the Writer

Pastor Mike Novotny has served God's people in full-time ministry since 2007 in Madison and, most recently, at The CORE in Appleton, Wisconsin. He also serves as the lead speaker for Time of Grace, where he shares the good news about Jesus through television, print, and online platforms. Mike loves seeing people grasp the depth of God's amazing grace and unstoppable mercy. His wife continues to love him (despite plenty of reasons not to), and his two daughters open his eyes to the love of God for every Christian. When not talking about Jesus or dating his wife/girls, Mike loves playing soccer, running, and reading.

About Time of Grace

Time of Grace is an independent, donor-funded ministry that connects people to God's grace—his love, glory, and power—so they realize the temporary things of life don't satisfy. What brings satisfaction is knowing that because Jesus lived, died, and rose for all of us, we have access to the eternal God—right now and forever.

To discover more, please visit timeofgrace.org or call 800.661.3311.

Help share God's message of grace!

Every gift you give helps Time of Grace reach people around the world with the good news of Jesus. Your generosity and prayer support take the gospel of grace to others through our ministry outreach and help them experience a satisfied life as they see God all around them.

Give today at timeofgrace.org/give or by calling 800.661.3311.

Thank you!